ID0684697

Tidal
Wave

First Edition 2020
Published in the United States of America
Printed by Spencer Printing
ISBN 978-1-7355148-0-2
Publisher's Cataloging-In-Publication Data
(Prepared by The Donohue Group, Inc.)

Names: Lee, Dennis H., 1946- author.
Title: Tidal wave / Dennis H. Lee.
Description: First edition. | Baltimore, MD : Passager Books, 2020.
Identifiers: ISBN 9781735514802
Subjects: LCSH: Life--Poetry. | Coming of age--Poetry. | Aging--Poetry. |
    LCGFT: Poetry.
Classification: LCC PS3612.E34267 T54 2020 | DDC 811/.6--dc23

Passager Books
7401 Park Heights Avenue
Baltimore, Maryland 21208
www.passagerbooks.com

Tidal
Wave

DENNIS H. LEE

Passager Books
Baltimore, MD
2020

Acknowledgments

Alimentum: The Literature of Food: "Arpeggio"

Descant: "Fortune Cookie"

Journal of Medical Humanities: "Blood Room"

pacificREVIEW: A West Coast Arts Review: "Coney Island – July 4, 1952"

Passager: "Recycling"

for Donna

Destiny came down to an island, centuries ago, and summoned three of the inhabitants before him.

What would you do, asked Destiny, *if I told you that tomorrow this island will be completely inundated by an immense tidal wave?*

The first man, who was a cynic, said, *Why, I would eat, drink, carouse and make love all night long!*

The second man, who was a mystic, said, *I would go to the sacred grove with my loved ones and make sacrifices to the gods and pray without ceasing.*

And the third man, who loved reason, thought for a while, confused and troubled, and said, *Why, I would assemble our wisest men and begin at once to study how to live under water.*

Leo Rosten, *Captain Newman, M.D.*

Table of Contents

Tidal
Wave

Coney Island – July 4, 1952

Uncle Nathan rubs back the hair
over blue numbers,
chants Hebrew psalms,
then slips away to a heavy wooden chair
planted to face the fence
where my father watches a ballgame
through slats that will never be fixed.
On its way to taunt Uncle Nathan,
Grandma's beef smoke
oils the undersides of leaves on her favorite maple.

My father sprawls out, holds a sun reflector,
feet dug into sand
down to where it's cool,
Grandma's maple, parchment-dry.
Chicken fat soaks into brown paper bags
three floors up on the clean white kitchen windowsill.
I sit on the fire escape with kosher chicken and comics.
Grandma speaks Yiddish into the soup.
Tonight's sky will be brighter than the Ferris wheel.

Measuring Our Time

I pushed a grocery cart
peaked with soda bottles
and large brown beer bottles
emptied the day before
at a Brooklyn supermarket construction site.

The smelly deli-counter guy
shoved the back door open
like a madman –
after I'd banged on it for half an hour
with a rock –
and paid me

two cents for each sixteen-ounce soda
and a nickel a beer bottle.

I would mount my Schwinn from the curb
and get off the same way, but this time
swivel-jumped and ran and got off
pulling back on the wide handlebars
digging my heels into street.

I grouped nine quarters, eighteen dimes, and seven nickels
onto the glass counter
for a set of four Hungarian triangles,

patted them –
glassine-enveloped in my front-button pocket –

zoomed down the asphalt ramp
that split Lloyd's row house
from his backyard
and scratched on his garage door like a dog
to negotiate for his 1952 mint Hawaiian

still in its clear plastic sleeve
as my son transfers the Canadian Georges
into a book he has made at school,
carefully drawing a box around each stamp
with India ink,
as if to measure the permanence
of this collection.

Grandma's Buttons

Ticking on a wooden sewing table
in the parlor, spilling onto
the floor – getaways – and
I creep down, head between
the legs of the table. Above
me the drawer and its wonderful
mechanism that lets it slide – open / close –
and I'm feeling for the buttons –
flat wishbones, rounded
ones that feel like wood
that aged wood – and above
the thunder. Grandma's pouring buttons
into a round metal tin that held
butter cookies from Aunt
Celia, who painted her chalked face
with pink powder – or so it seemed
to me.

Leaning in my tired seat

falling down the tube of sleep
in a subway, screech-like sounds
smell of electric spark,
to Brooklyn, Coney Island,
last stop, where the Mermaid Avenue bus turns
around to go back to 37th Street from whence I came.

My mother, a little child dressed-up in white,
even white shoes, holds a Charlotte Russe, white
cup in her little hand. She has not taken a lick, nor
a bite, as she looks up at her mother's mother who
has opened a white umbrella to shield the sun on this summer day
just outside Sea Gate (that special gated community).

Her mother has crossed the last street to join them
for their walk along the Sea Gate fence toward the beach, the boardwalk.
Up the wooden ramp they go, Mother's mother's white boot heels
clapping thinly against the planks a steady slow walk up. And Mother
can see the round thick silver railing that runs along the boardwalk's edge
where it looks out over the wide expanse of beach to the Atlantic Ocean.

Grandpa is sitting on a bench there sleeping, dreaming of Russia,
of cows in a small fenced pasture along the road he walks carrying
eggs in a basket for his grandmother who had kind blues eyes. Sad,
but kind. Her husband had just died and she was now alone it seemed.
But Grandfather would sit with her and listen to the story of how they met,

how a matchmaker came to her father with the news, and how they made
a life together, not really her dream.

And the smell of electric track and the hissing of machine
penetrates and brings back this place again where unconscious
and conscious need to meet to bring time to life.

Arpeggio

I liked to tear clumps of challah
from the round braided pile of bread,
squinching the piece in my hand to help
leverage the tearing, then watch it
slowly rise back to fluff.

My grandmother made Maxwell House coffee
in a percolator, also filled me a wide mouthed
glass cup, put in three teaspoons of
sugar, then slowly poured in heavy cream
so I could watch it spiral and cloud its way down.

Why do they call it heavy? It floats
until it's pulled down by the black hot coffee. If
it goes sour it tries to warn by leaving pieces
floating on top – floating!

When I was a teenager I'd go to the movies
on Friday night with friends, then to the diner
for malteds, coffee and bagels. Mark once asked
"Mind if I dip?" and reached across the table
to drown his half bagel in my coffee.

I don't know what's become of Mark. My grandmother
is gone so long that every memory of her is a wonder.
Don't know what habits or
nuances I can pass to my grandchildren. Maybe they'll
turn everything said into a song.

So what, you wet your pants.

There was this older gentleman at the country
club who played middle-of-the-road golf,
but was always polite, never cursed. He had
been a professional his entire career after graduating
from Yale. His wife was glorious, and hosted many
a tea party in their backyard. Three children had moved
to different countries, and the youngest, a boy, stayed
and lived in New York.

This man traveled to Long Island to meet with a psychic.
The room was filled with others like him – seeking a lost
relative or friend. The little woman who spoke with the
departed sort of danced around the room – darting here
then there, asking questions to specific members of the group
like "Do you know Wolfie? Does that name sound familiar?"
If she got a response she would stop and go on conversing
and relating information to the group member – and asking
more questions.

"*I don't care that you wet your pants. It doesn't matter now.*
Do you know about this?" She was standing in front of the man,
looking at him, then at the people on either side of him. "*Don't
just sit there,* she's saying, *I don't care anymore.*
Who here knows this person? It's a very strong presence."
No one spoke. And the little woman
moved on.

Tea and Cream with a Coffee Bean

"Tea and cream with a coffee bean."
"What?" "Tea and cream with a coffee bean,
please." "Is that your order?" "Yes."
"That's it. For now. Can I keep the menu?"
"Do you mean take it?" "No. Just here – while
I'm here at the table." "Sure. So – is that
something you saw on the menu – on our menu?"
"What?" "Tea and cream with a coffee bean."
"No actually. I did / do see tea on the menu. And
I imagine you serve cream – for the tea. I am
hoping you may have a coffee bean in the kitchen.
If so – could I have that on the side?" "So – you want
tea with cream and the coffee bean on the side?"
"Actually, I would like a cup of hot water with a
tea bag, cream – possibly in a little pitcher or such, so
I can pour it in to my liking, and yes – the coffee bean
on the side." "You would not want the coffee bean in the
tea?" "You mean the hot water?" "Yes." "No."
"Hello. Is there some trouble here – at this table?"
"No sir. This customer just wants a special order."
"Something that is not on our menu?" "Sort of not."
"I have just ordered tea and cream with a coffee bean.
The tea is certainly on the menu. I assume the cream can
be ordered with the tea. Like milk or cream with coffee. And
because I do see coffee on the menu, I was hoping to get
a coffee bean. If you see that as extra, then please charge me."
"This customer makes perfect sense. Please! No problem.
Enjoy your meal – or rather your tea – with your coffee bean."
"And my cream – thank you!"

Recycling

I start to receive mail in jars. See-through
glass bottles. "Has this
ever happened to you?" I ask the
mailman. "No," he says. "It's got the right
postage. Are you the addressee?" "Yes," I say,
"I am."

The first jar contains a note from Maude
Lacinne. I don't know a Maude Lacinne. The
note is brief. She finds it wonderful. I've
made her so happy. She has lived alone
in her apartment for seventeen years –
has never left. My magazines
have let her see outside again.
(I have no idea about such magazines!)
She has lost weight.
She has married the elevator man. She
is moving from her apartment on the third floor
to an apartment on the seventeenth
floor. *Love and kisses and God bless.*

The jar is quite functional. It's
large enough to hold my rice. I wash it
and dry it and leave it on the counter, half-filled
with white grains. I put her
note on my refrigerator door. The
next day I receive two more jars.
The postman hand-delivers them to my porch.

He is concerned that they might break
in the mailbox. "Beautiful weather. Have
a nice day," he says. "Yes, thank you."
They look like a matching set.

These two jars are smaller than the first. One
is from Aubrey Spencil, who has bought a new
dog like the one on page sixty-seven of the
June Whittlebrook Catalog. The second is from
an anonymous admirer who likens himself
to the tailor in my article on skiing.

I continue to receive jars in the mail with
notes (and references to my magazines
and articles). There are too many jars now, so
I bring them to a local flea market and place
them on tables where they look comfortable. I have
put something in each jar, a note containing thoughts
about Maude's weight loss, her marriage,
dog food coupons.

I begin to mail my old newspapers
to random names in the phonebook.
I attach a note to each, thanking the name
for sending a jar. I explain
how I now use this particular jar to hold my fish recipes
or how fresh my rice has stayed.

Frankenmatzoh

I don't know what had impelled me such.
I had awakened from a bad sleep.
It was furnace noises, or that of snowplows
scratching across the macadam surface
of the street outside. The back and forth
and shoveling sounds of the strange looking
caged tractors that worked at night.

True my sleeps had been poor for nights.
I had woken in sweats or just by car doors
slammed by neighbors who had stayed out very late.
Maybe by that dark grey cat with one white paw
who lurked. Maybe just by dreams of it all,
or by having no dreams at all.

Why I had saved one box of matzoh after each Passover
for six years is no reason to question what I did.
Nor is it your business to even concern over.
But I was awake. And I took one slice of matzoh
from each box. And I stacked them on the counter
in the kitchen next to the refrigerator.
And I conjured a thought.

Carefully I broke off a piece of matzoh
from year one. I worked along the perforations,
but the matzoh broke unevenly. "Bad matzoh!"
I thought, and threw the rest away. I tried the same
with year two. "Bad matzoh!" Year three and four.

Year five and six. "All bad matzohs!" None would break evenly
for me.

All these pieces and crumbled mess! I tried to
put them all side by side – the long broken pieces.
But they were jagged, ill formed. They did not
create a square – perfect or otherwise. A horn
began outside. A plow must have joggled a car
and that incessant horn began its bark. I held
my ears. It must have been for minutes. And
I saw what I needed to do.

The horn stopped. I opened the refrigerator
door and found my round carton of whipped butter.
I spooned out large lumps into a bowl. With my
fingers I rubbed and pasted the butter along
the edges of the matzoh pieces – pasted them
together to make a slice of matzoh again
from the six years of perforated broken
pieces. It took much time and concentration.
But there it was, my Frankenmatzoh. And
I ate it and drank a cup of warm milk
and went to sleep again. And I remember
dreaming of kittens.

My Doctor's Dog

1
My doctor's dog
is quite efficient. He brings
the clipboard over to new patients
or to those of us who need to update
our information. I don't mind
the bite marks on the forms. But
I do mind the slobber on the pen
(although the office now has tissue boxes
distributed for us complainers). Often
he'll lie down and put his head on your shoe.
(I really don't like it when he sits and scratches
or sniffs all over my legs – no,
it's not cute!).

2
So I'm out looking again.
(I sure hope I don't get sick)
(maybe I should make appointments,
given their earliest is three weeks out.)
A coworker told me about a doctor
who rides a small horse into the exam room.
His nurse announces his imminent arrival
with great fanfare. (I really don't believe it.)

3

I finally found a pretty good doctor. He
does have chickens who run
loose in the front yard squawking – but
the wait is short.
Problem is his license to practice
might get suspended.
So I have begun self-healing (this may be
the American solution to health care!)
I only give myself fifteen minutes for diagnosis,
and I always prescribe ice cream –
but I vary the flavor.

Gut Music

Beethoven's wife was a great house cleaner.
It may be well documented that she would
push her vacuum cleaner (one of
the best on the market) near the piano
to suck up all those cookie crumbs
and cigarette ashes created by the composer
during his long arduous sessions
at the piano. He would just lift
his feet and keep on tinkling the keys.
But not much has been written
about her bad cooking. She did
not combine (shall we say compose) complementary
ingredients. Sadly this led
to Beethoven's famous bouts
of indigestion. Of course they influenced his music –
and we are now blessed by her bad cooking
and his good taste.

My analyst

has no email address. He does not carry
a cell phone. There is no window in his office,
and only one chair.

He has no desk really, just a small table,
like a coffee table – to put his coffee on. He
writes with a pencil on a yellow pad.

The only item I have really taken notice of
is a small yellow pencil sharpener – the kind
I used to have in a pencil case in grade school.

I have focused in on that. He told me his mother
gave it to him, and not to his brother. This is
something he has brought up often in our sessions.

Sometimes when I sense tenseness in his face, when
he can't stop fiddling with the sharpener, I ask him
about the day his mother gave it to him.

When he repeats the story of that day, I can see the skin
on his forehead relax. He looks at the outside wall (as
if through a window he wishes were there).

I know I am reaching him – he has brought another cup
into the room. Soon I believe he will ask me if I
would like some coffee.

Take-out Order (on the phone)

A side of salmon please.
Yes, a side of salmon please.
With broccoli please, not the peas.
Yes, broccoli, please.
Right. Salmon but no peas, please.
And a steak with peas. Yes, peas.
And another please.
A steak with peas.
Yes two. Two steaks with peas.
Right, the salmon with no peas. Please.
That's it. Our name is Lees, yes Lees.
Twenty minutes is fine. Yes, Lees.
No this is not a joke, I'll be right there.
And remember cook the steaks with care.
Both medium, but with care.
The salmon too with care.
Okay thanks. I'll be right there.
No. Not a joke. I'll be right there.
Right. Two steaks and salmon cooked with care
Twenty minutes – yes – I'll be right there.
Thank you. Good-bye. I'll be right there.

The Barking Woman

She lived in a house attached to another house which was
attached to another house – and so on and so forth.
And whenever she was there she was barking. She could be heard
barking at her children – and they in turn could be heard barking.
In the morning, the afternoon, and evening, she would be barking.
At night the barking would stop. But in the morning – barking.
Outside her house – barking with her children (and they would leave her
as they continued their barking, and she too – barking). And on and on
it went. Her barking would sometimes be louder and accompanied
by slamming – and the children too, slamming. And jumping. Jumping
and slamming while barking. One day one of her neighbors noticed smoke
drifting out of her front windows, but when she was told
she started slamming harder and barking louder.
So everyone tried to avoid her, just stay out of her way.
And the smoking continued. And the barking continued.
And the slamming continued.
One day she bought a small quiet dog who would not bark.
She spent days and weeks and months training that dog, but
he would not bark. He would sit up and look at her, wag his tail
while the children ran around slamming –
but he would not bark.
She left the house in a huff with her children – they were slamming
and barking and she drove off, and was gone for hours
– hours. And the little dog began pacing around the house,
trying to see out of a window.
He scratched and scratched at the bottom of the front door.
And someone said that on that day, that little dog began barking,
and barking, and barking,
and has not stopped barking.

Vacationing with the Olympic Team in the Andes

Part 1

Our first breakfast at the hotel started far earlier
than I expected, but it was the variety and quantities
of food that were most reportable. Of all the Olympians
D_, L_, and S_ were the only ones I thought
had a light breakfast. M_ and R_ each ate so many pancakes
that I lost count. The pancakes were served on super-large platters
placed onto the two ends of each of the long picnic-type tables. Eggs
(scrambled) were brought out in large bowls and served continuously
during breakfast by what I called the "egg-team," a group of waiters
and waitresses all dressed in yellow shirts embossed with a black "O."
In speaking with the hotel "Nutrition Staff" management later, I was told
that so many eggs were anticipated that other hotels in the area provided
fifteen percent of their eggs, and people in a 25-mile radius self-rationed.
(I plan another piece entitled "Andes Eggs for the Olympians.")
E_ kept ordering peaches and sweet cream
(later I found that the kitchen staff actually complained).
It was a simple dish, but was consumed by E_ for over 68 minutes straight
in what looked to me like an "event." I was told by a few of his friends
that this "breakfast habit" caused his divorce
(actually an annulment after research), and that two spiritual advisors
spoke to the couple about the "issue." There was sausage, rolls, gallons
of orange juice, tomato juice, grapefruit juice, and at least six glasses
of fresh-squeezed-pickle-juice (true, you heard it here!).
Many of the Olympians wandered into the gift shop after finishing breakfast
while waiting for the others.

N_ had a fascination with donkeys which was shared by M_, L_, F_, and W_.
They were all collecting donkey statues, donkey greeting cards,
donkey sweatshirts, and other donkey-related souvenirs,
a group fetish that I hope to explain in Part 2.

"Before you write from the heart,

we will need you to take a stress
test." "What?" "We will inject
a dye that will provide us visual
markers that show when you begin
writing from the heart and when you stop."
"I don't believe that that is possible."
"Our tests have always been an accurate
measure. We will discuss our findings
with you at a conference two weeks
after your test. This provides our doctors,
staff-writers, and editors time
to analyze your results." "What if
you find that I do not always write
from the heart?" "That would be
consistent with our findings,
and will have no effect on the content
of any subsequent rejection slips we send
you. Thank you for your time, and
remember to fast before the test."

Lunch

The accountants are talking baseball
or Little League. I don't know sports,
not the way you talk about them.
This table will never be me – I'm "IT"
and they just want to ask me about
spreadsheet tricks (I don't know any).

I'd never sit with the secretaries.
They know too much, and I don't
want to become part of that. Also
why would I sit with a bunch of
women, I'm married, you can see
where this could go.

The salespeople are ridiculous.
I couldn't possibly keep up with
the stories. They go topic to topic
and every story is great – or needs
to be. Not for me. I'm here to eat.
"Oh yeah and the best meal I ever had
was –" blah, blah, blah.

The guys from the plant are too
down-to-earth. They don't just know,

they do. Don't be a screwup at this
table. Too risky. They might just eat
you (probably not).

I sit with one buddy from IT.
We bull about whatever
stupid thing we've been told to do.
Not the great stuff of programming.
We reference movie actors in the wrong
movies, try to remember the plots.
And there it is, "Paul Newman ate
all the eggs!"

The hand sanitizer at my new bar

is right next to the bowl of peanuts.
That taste comes right through.
My scotch won't kill it. Not even
the jalapeños. Luckily the salt
on the bottom of the peanut bowl
is starting to numb my tongue. But
now I can't pronounce properly.
The old plumber to my right
just poured that sanitizer all over
his hands before grabbing those
peanuts (lucky for me, cause I
just heard him tell this morning's story).
But that taste is ruining my peanuts!

The man who had nothing wrong

stumped the doctors for years. In New York
at the great hospital a wise learned doctor
with yellowed diplomas on his walls and the ability to
recite from merely an x-ray told the man with nothing
wrong that he needed a series of tests, and he was there
himself to tell the man that there was nothing
that these tests resolved. So he sent the man to a specialist
uptown. The man went dutifully and sat while the specialist
read the tests – this doctor who paced and sat
and looked out of his high story windows down to the cars in the street
told the man of a great doctor at a great hospital in the Midwest.
The man traveled, stayed at a hotel, then entered the hospital in the Midwest
and was shuffled from his room to tests on different floors given by serious
or funny technicians who assured him that results would be forthcoming.
But the team of great doctor-specialists offered him no conclusions. They
said that they saw "*nothing.*" And one of these doctors, the most special
of the specialists, said he knew of a very great doctor in the South who had
dealt with such cases, and that he was sure that *he* would find *something*!
The man traveled again, this time very hopeful
after the special-specialist's enthusiasm.
And the great doctor was very hopeful after the initial visit
that he would find something – that he "always" found something.
So again, days of tests. But this time far more invasive.
A special probe was used while nuclear drugs were IV'd into a vein,
and he was lowered into a grand machine that was new and large
and more expensive than all the other machines. And he was scanned digitally
at great speeds with wide bandwidth, and the great doctor remained
behind a glass window in a room filled with computers

that overlooked the grand machine. Two days later, as the man was recovering from the effects of the grand machine and wonder drugs, the great, "great" doctor walked into his room smiling. "That's it!" he said. "It's conclusive! The scans show nothing visible!
I have spoken to all your previous specialists on a 3-hour conference call, and we have determined that this is not a physical ailment!
I will be giving you the name of a specialist in the West
who has worked at the best hospitals in the East,
and he will begin a battery of what we call mind-evaluations.
This is in fact the place where we are *sure* to provide a diagnosis of *something*!"

Candle in the Universe

We sat at our desks.
Tony kept clicking his inkwell.
Miss Torpo would turn and look his way,
and he'd stop instantaneously – then start again.
But she was distracted. Mr. Ostenbruner was setting up.

He had placed a white candle in the middle of her
completely cleared desk top. He was now placing balls
at different lengths around the candle – a baseball,
a ping-pong ball, a tennis ball – and some other rubbery-looking
balls (the kind little kids play with).

And he would step back – and back – and then
to the desk and moving the balls (ah, even a soccer ball).
And some of us were watching, and some of us were talking,
and Miss Torpo would rap a piece of chalk quickly on the blackboard
to signal – *shut up!*

Mr. Ostenbruner was the man we would see in the halls
on a ladder changing a lightbulb or painting over a door frame.
Or outside fixing a loose door-closer. Or in the Boys room putting
a sign over a sink or toilet "Broken. Do not use."
He could appear almost anywhere – just walk in during class,
fix something, then walk out.

Now here he was in our class – still in his white overalls –
about to teach us something. And again Miss Torpo rapped
the chalk fast, and sharp, and loud – and we all stopped

and looked forward. "Mr. Ostenbruner will now bring us
the Universe," she announced. "But first I need volunteers
to bring down the window shades."

Four boys jumped up
and each began pulling hard and fast
on the cords connected to the shades. And there was
terrible squeaking and rolling noises and dust began
to float in the air – beautiful dust particles captured by the sun
still streaking past the shades where they didn't quite fit.

And Mr. Ostenbruner lit the candle, and we all watched
as the flame flickered and a thin stream of dark smoke
rose up toward the very high ceiling. He pointed at the candle.
"The sun," he said. And he was sure of it. He picked up the baseball.
"Earth," he said. And he began to walk around Miss Torpo's desk.
Round and round.

Louie, the kid in the back row, was waving his hand
back and forth and making moaning sounds. "What
is it, Louie?" said Miss Torpo. "I have to go to the bathroom."
He said, "But I don't want to miss the baseball going around the
candle." "No." Mr. Ostenbruner said pointing. "Sun. And here,
Earth." "Okay!" Louie yelled as he ran out of the room. "I just
have to pee, so I'll be back before the sun burns out." And we
giggled, and watched the black smoke rise. And Mr. Ostenbruner sat down.

The Statue

I first noticed it staring at me
when I looked up from my sandwich.
It was a kind of glare, a disdain
for ham and cheese, or mustard
that had dripped on one knee.

I tried to clean the yellow gook
with one of the napkins and some spit.
And I noticed the furrowed brow,
a head that was starting to shake
a disapproving "No!"

His right arm was raised in a fist.
(So glad he was stuck fast!)
"You silly schmuck!" I said.
And an old woman pushing a carriage
pushed faster.

Again he scowled. His eyes were no eyes
at all – like stones. Ah! They are stone!
I'm trying to clean mustard
from my pants. He thinks
I'm a jerk. He's an ass – made of stone!

I got up. A splotch on my left knee.
I dumped the bag and garbage left
from my lunch into a wire waste bucket.
But first I squeezed some mustard from a packet

onto that bastard's toes – right over the dried bird poop.

"Grab ash!"

I can't remember the stadium steps
at the Hoolings Bay High School football
field. Orange. I believe they were painted
orange. But Simador Kliven-Jay always
seemed to be there at the wrong time to
yell at us (who was he anyway to yell at us?).
Orkin and Mel and Nuzzy and Little-Pete and
Moonshine and I liked to meet under the stadium
seats and talk about women. Nuzzy smoked
unfiltered cigarettes and lit his matches with one hand.
Little-Pete coughed near smoke and was always moving
away from anyone who lit up. Mel smoked menthols.
But Moonshine smoked the worst-smelling, skinny cigars.

Simador was the exchange student. I don't know
what country he was from. Nuzzy called him KJ.
We saw him all over doing some kind of clean-up thing.
I don't think he had to. Orkin, our smart friend, said
that Simador *Needed to express his grand appreciation
for being allowed in this country*. Mel thought he was nuts.
Anyway it was a very still spring day, not a leaf was blowing,
and Moonshine was trying to break his all-time record for
not losing the ash from the end of his cigar, and well, you know,
Simador, he just kept pointing and yelling at Moonshine.

Shoppin' Sheryl

Into the car, off in a dash,
through the circle with never a tarry,
whisking round curves not for faint hearts,
locking into a waiting space.

This is not a scene in which to lounge –
grab your hat and get!
You can feel the wind,
even in the still mall air.

Like the starts and stops of a Brooklyn bus
that can fell even the most balanced gymnast.
Have your wits about
if you ride this spree!

Ah, a pause!
Turning of the shoe
to the concentration of a Buddha.
Turning every shoe,
as Buddhas come and go.

Just as I start to relax,
she jumps back
into the traffic, mall traffic,
shoppers' traffic.

There she goes!
I see her flag, the white turban.

The shell game now,
blouses on the rack – ack, ack, ack, ack.

Shoes again – and again!
Pants, blouses, skirts, sweat suits,
Pots –
. . . *Pots?*

"Why'd we buy a pot?"
"Good buy!"
"Good-bye."

Blood Room

The little girl fascinated by your nail polish
watched as your eyes stayed down on nervous knitting.

I couldn't help staring –
shy smiles
and burying that tiny flesh head
into her mother's lap.

At the hanging of the blood
you worked fresh wool, knitting needles in your hands,
IV needles stuck into your flesh.

On the other side of the room
that tiny head again, turning so many ways to sorry smiles.
You just knit, knit, knit.

On Dark Wings

I held her hand,
not waiting for death,
but in anticipation of Colorado
or Canada, a vacation
filled with expectation.

I held her hand
with the courage I would give our children,
with the courage to face doctors
who, like reporters,
just tell the story
(there's always a story).

I held her hand
as if I expected pain to be afraid,
to run away
when it saw us.

I held her hand
as it swelled with poison
that dripped into her arm through a needle
connected to theories of doctors
who once prescribed leeches.

I held her dead hand,
the gold meaningless band
shining in sunlight
that couldn't warm her skin,
couldn't give answers,
couldn't even ask the questions.

Fortune Cookie

I cracked open a fortune cookie
and a great song began to play,
and everyone looked,

and two dancers began to dance,
and I was one,
and everyone smiled,

and one of the dancers let go,
and I couldn't dance anymore,
and the music stopped,

and the onlookers began to cry.

I Wish Now I Could Have Buried You

I buried my yellow parakeet
in a grave I dug
with my small red shovel.

I placed her soft body into a clean hole
dug with care
each pebble removed by tiny fingers.

I covered her by hand
head last
mounded and patted the grave.

I placed a special stone
to mark her history
in my memory.

They buried you with pomp and religion.

I only watched and mourned
stood still
steeped in silent rules.

Eating Crab

I have been tearing through the Bible,
looking for those morsels people
talk about, people with a taste
for Bible and for "God."

This is difficult work, and I have
found very little to chew on. Most
of this stuff I'm not able to extract,
and the little that reaches my mouth –
well, I'm not sure it's worth the effort.

A few little strands, sweet and succulent,
and I draw them through my lips slowly,
savoring. My hands need washing.
I do not wear a bib. My plate
is filled with cracked discards.

Redundant Lives

Lean as a canoe.
All she needs is a little varnish.
The mirror holds her prisoner
in a room that sings her wedding vows.

A ton of iron can ruin a plan.
His big buckled legs dead beneath
a present still kept
polished in a closed garage.

Venetian blinds
screen the street life from her view.

They'd been brave as
ducks beneath a clear surface.
Born between grace
and a slap in the face.

Now she waits for June-Trees,
throws coffee grounds to feed her garden,

and his.

Stopped in the Midst of My Continuation

It could have been when
driving my car into a spot at the mall –
slowly so as not to disturb the two birds,
one blue, one red, as they both pulled on
the same twig – I was interrupted by the
sound from a speaker on top of a truck
(like a large ice cream van) announcing
the finals of a high school cheerleader
competition in the park behind the mall,
and the scurrying of teenagers through
the parking lot (to get a good viewing
spot?), screaming to each other, when
one boy dropped a bag of marbles (marbles?)
and they began rolling everywhere, so a few
of us stopped to help him gather the marbles
(and to prevent anyone from slipping on
them) and the woman next to me did slip
and fell hard and I dropped my marbles
and kneeled down to help her (her foot
looked very twisted) but she began
to sit herself up, so I stood to stop
a car that was barreling down to get
into a spot that just opened when *BAM*
another car pulling out of a spot hit it
in the side door and the marbled woman
was now standing (I guess she didn't
really twist her ankle) and began screaming
to a friend of hers about two rows down.
So I got into my car to leave.

Or was it when I was stuck
in traffic listening to how Maya
Angelou checked into a hotel room
with yellow pads to write each of
her seven autobiographies, when
a cop slammed down on my hood
with his palm and angrily pointed
for me to pull to the side (was I
daydreaming?) (no, my inspection
sticker was out-of-date) and wrote
me a ticket that would force a hectic
expensive court appearance.

But I actually think it was when I was getting
out of my car in front of my house,
waving to a certain neighbor who usually
walked her snappy dog too close
when I realized that the loud rumbling sound
was emanating from *my* basement,
and the tennis balls I had left in the dryer
had walked the dryer almost halfway
to the other side of the laundry room.

Dryer Sheets

"Hi Mrs. Bloom, what are you doing in the yard
with dryer sheets," "Oh these are wonderful,
they smell so much better than my roses. I just
put a box of sheets on sticks among my rose bushes."
"Ahhh, you are right these really smell.
Smelling like a rose was always overrated."

"Look, here comes Gladys." "Wow, I could smell
those from across the street, they smell stronger
than my laundry!" "Mrs. Bloom has added dryer sheets
to her rose bushes to get rid of that rosy smell." "Wow
it works! I can't even smell my clothes, let alone
all my perfume (I used half the bottle!)"

"Paul, my neighbor rubs dryer sheets on his baby.
He says it's much better than baby powder smell. And
so grown up!" "These dryer sheets should shoo away
any rodents from my garden – they really stink!" "I'll
bet the Garden Society would love to hear about this!"

"Hi everybody, I was just doing my laundry when
this new smell came right though my closed
windows. I had to throw extra dryer sheets in my wash
to cover it up!" "It is dryer sheets!" "No! These are roses!"
"No more!" said Mrs. Bloom. "Better!"

We're sorry to keep you waiting.

But all of our staff are helping others.
There are 3 callers ahead of you.
Bill had quite a weekend. His mother
has the flu and he needed to tend
to the needs of his aging father.

We're sorry to keep you waiting.
Janet is traveling this week. She's
in California helping her daughter Ethyl
get settled in school. Ethyl is a sophomore,
her first year was nearly terrible.

We're sorry to keep you waiting.
There are 2 callers in front of you.
Our secretary had her hair colored yesterday
and she believes she's having an allergic
reaction to the dye. Joan is applying
cold compresses to her forehead.

We're sorry to keep you waiting.
The front door to our office was locked
this morning. Many of us had to wait
in the rain. Sam ran and got us all coffee.
He's on the phone right now helping
another customer.

We're sorry to keep you waiting.
There are 1 callers in front of you.

Mary is holding a ladder for Mabel
who is replacing a light bulb. Henson
is handing her a new bulb, John is guarding
the switch, and Louis is manning
the circuit breaker.

We're sorry to keep you waiting.
But all of our staff are helping others.
There are 0 callers ahead of you.
We're sorry to keep you waiting.
But all of our staff are helping others.
There are 0 callers ahead of you.

Tidal Wave

White Lake is what we called it. But
it was really Kauneonga Lake. Our hotel was
the Rosedale. We began going when I was very young,
maybe eight. We knew the owner (my parents
did, and I did too). The Catskills.

The hotel was very simple. The meals too.
But the lake! The water was like drinking
water. That clear. A wooden dock
with steps that led into the water. It was shallow.
Even I could walk, and walk out, on the hard sandy bottom.

Then there was a drop. You knew before you reached it.
A sure slope began, and you could just turn around and walk
back. Or you begin swimming right from the dock steps.
Standing on the dock after sunrise on a calm day,
the lake was like a mirror. Not a ripple. Filled with sky.

I began fishing there. My father taught me. We
caught sunnies. When I let my line down
into the water they surged to eat the bait. It was
hard not to catch one. I kept them alive in a pail
and let them loose again. I was very good at this.

As I got older I began to fish for bass using lures.
The water was so clear that I could see a fish
thirty feet out and try to cast in front of it. I only

fished just after sunrise, or just before sunset. It
was at sunset that it happened.

The whole lake was shaped like a baby rattle.
There was a large roundish area in the north
and a large roundish area in the south joined
by a straight area about one mile wide. At the dock
I looked across a two-mile span of water.

During the day the lake was busy with motorboats,
water skiers, canoes, rowboats, sail boats, swimmers.
There were even people fishing – on boats, and from shore.
But just after sunrise, silence. And just before sunset, peace.
I shut the clicking of my reel off because of the noise.

I was casting and reeling in. I could hear my lure click
into the lake when it landed. Casting and reeling in.
And then a new sound. Faint at first, but growing
in intensity. I kept reeling in and listening for
where the sound was coming from – ever louder.

My part of the sky was still clear. My part of the
lake still. But out there, toward the middle
of the lake it was dark. And what looked like a wall
of water, a giant wave, was coming right at me. I
dropped my rod and ran for the hotel.

I could feel my heart pound. I remembered a wave
at Coney Island when I was about six that lifted
me and carried me up the beach. People screaming.
Water began to cover me. Rain water. A deluge of rain.
I was running so incredibly wet and happy. That's it.

Thank you Donna J. Gelagotis Lee, my poet wife, who met me at a small poetry group almost thirty years ago where I was trying to write poems to my first wife and childhood sweetheart Sheryl, who died at 43. You have encouraged and inspired me and pointed me toward this wonderful experience (thank you Passager!). Thanks to my mother Sylvia who introduced me to poetry when I was six. Thanks to my grandmother Gussie from Coney Island who was always there. And to my mother-in-law Dee, who is here now. Thank you to my father who taught me generosity and introduced me to Broadway, and thank you to my grandfather. Thank you to my friends and family and extended California family, who listened to my ramblings and read my poems and have always been so warm and generous. And to my children and grandchildren. Love is really wonderful.

I would also like to give thanks to the experiences in and the people of Brooklyn and Kaunconga Lake (White Lake). I was really blessed to grow up in Brooklyn in the 50's and 60's where for 60 cents I could subway to the United Nations and back home, I could walk to the beach and boardwalk, bike to my grandmother's house on Coney Island to go on the rides or to fish on the rocks in the Atlantic Ocean, I could take my date for a ride on the Staten Island Ferry. And working in the Catskills was really dancing at great hotels to the music of terrific bands, water skiing, fishing, and keeping the guests' teenage children (people my age) happy.

I would also like to thank Kendra, Mary, Pantea, Christine and the folks at Passager for giving me such a terrific experience during this year of 2020. Wow!

Dennis H. Lee grew up in Brooklyn and would spend Shabbat at his grandparents' home just outside of Seagate, on Coney Island. His parents owned a stationery store on 44th Street in the theatre district of Manhattan, where he met many actors. He graduated from the College of the Sequoias, with a degree in Electronics and he served in the U.S. Navy, part of that time on the U.S.S. Enterprise. In the 1960s, he sang with the doo-wop group *The Nocturnes*, which once followed Richie Havens at the Cafe Wha? in NYC. He worked as a computer software engineer for many years. Dennis and his wife, Donna, co-founded the Delaware Valley Poets Reading Series in Princeton, which continued for more than twenty years.

The Henry Morgenthau III First Book Poetry Prize for a poet 70 or older

The prize honors Henry Morgenthau III, author of *A Sunday in Purgatory*, his first collection of poems at age 99. After a distinguished career as a writer and producer for public television, Mr. Morgenthau began writing poetry in his nineties, pursuing it with great seriousness and passion. He gave readings and book signings, enthralling audiences of all ages with his intelligence and wit, and fielded correspondence from people inspired by his poems. His audience was changed by him and he in turn by them. As he said, "to finally, in my nineties, after such a long and public life, be able to write and publish poems – to connect with other people from my deepest, truest self – was a gift. To be open to others in this way . . . I don't know why I waited so long."

Dennis H. Lee is the first recipient of this award.

In legends, the crane stands for longevity, peace, harmony, good fortune and fidelity. A high flyer, it is cherished for its ability to see both heaven and earth. These ancient, magnificent birds, so crucial in the wild as an "umbrella species," are now endangered and must be protected.

passager

Passager Books is dedicated to making public the passions of a generation vital to our survival.

If you would like to support Passager Books, please visit our website www.passagerbooks.com or email us at: editors@passagerbooks.com.

Tidal Wave was designed by Pantea Amin Tofangchi and typeset by Christine Drawl using Adobe InDesign. The pages are set in Adobe Garamond Pro and Gill Sans Nova.

The cover art is a 6" x 8" acrylic painting by C. V. Beatts titled "Turquoise" and is used with the artist's kind permission.

Printed in 2020 by Spencer Printing, Honesdale, PA.

Also from Passager Books

Prayers of Little Consequence
POEMS BY GILBERT ARZOLA

Days of Blue and Flame
POEMS BY SARAH YERKES

Taproot
POEMS BY KATHY MANGAN

The Uncorrected Eye
POEMS BY HARRY BAULD

Old Women Talking
POEMS BY WILDERNESS SARCHILD

Prickly Roses: Stories from a Life
A MEMOIR BY JOYCE ABELL

A Sunday in Purgatory
POEMS BY HENRY MORGENTHAU III

A Hinge of Joy, second edition
POEMS BY JEAN L. CONNOR

The Three O'Clock Bird
POEMS BY ANNE FRYDMAN

Finding Mr. Rightstein
A MEMOIR BY NANCY DAVIDOFF KELTON

Gathering the Soft
POEMS BY BECKY DENNISON SAKELLARIOU
ARTWORK BY TANDY ZORBA

Burning Bright: Celebrating Older Voices
POEMS, FICTION & MEMOIR
EDITED BY MARY AZRAEL & KENDRA KOPELKE

Hot Flash Sonnets
POEMS BY MOIRA EGAN

Improvise in the Amen Corner
POEMS & DRAWINGS BY LARNELL CUSTIS BUTLER

A Cartography of Peace
POEMS BY JEAN L. CONNOR